T0359817

Other titles in the UWAP Poetry series
(established 2016)

Malcolm

Leni Shilton

Leni Shilton is a poet, nurse, educator and researcher who has worked in Aboriginal adult education in the Northern Territory for 25 years. She has twice won the Northern Territory Literary Poetry and Essay Awards, and in 2015 was short-listed in the University of Canberra Poetry Prize. In February 2016 she completed a PhD in creative writing. *Walking with Camels – The Story of Bertha Strehlow* was published by UWA Publishing in 2018. Shilton's writing has appeared in anthologies and journals in Australia and internationally. She is a recipient of creative writing grants and international residencies and her work has appeared in exhibitions and been adapted for the stage. Leni is a founding member of Ptilotus Press, a small publishing initiative which promotes central Australian writing. She works for an Aboriginal women's organisation, the Ngaanyatjarra Pitjantjatjara Yunkunytjatjara Women's Council in Alice Springs, supporting community development women's groups.

Leni Shilton
Malcolm
a story in verse

Poetry

First published in 2019 by
UWA Publishing
Crawley, Western Australia 6009
www.uwap.uwa.edu.au

UWAP is an imprint of UWA Publishing,
a division of The University of Western Australia.

This book is copyright. Apart from any fair dealing
for the purpose of private study, research, criticism
or review, as permitted under the *Copyright Act 1968*,
no part may be reproduced by any process without
written permission. Enquiries should be made to
the publisher.

Copyright © Leni Shilton 2019
The moral right of the author has been asserted.
ISBN: 978-1-76080-053-6

 A catalogue record for this
book is available from the
National Library of Australia

Designed by Becky Chilcott, Chil3
Typeset in Lyon Text by Lasertype
Printed by McPherson's Printing Group

 uwapublishing

MIX
Paper from
responsible sources
FSC® C001695

For Chris

Chapter 1

On empty streets | January

Trams

The city yawns like a sleepy cat.
At this hour, lights glow yellow and hazy
on empty streets.

I keep my head down
on the No. 219 going home,
iPod pumping in my ears.

The ragged mob
shuffle on and off the tram.
I can pick the gear they're on –
but some don't need anything.
It's all in their heads,
they rave on and on
in the fluoro-lit air.

Metal tracks take us all
on the same path –
the tram driver
a million miles away
up front.

Home

It's early summer
so it's cold.

Joe cleared the crap from the fireplace
and tonight
after breaking up the table
we have our first fire.

It's smoky
and the room fills with haze,
a nice change
from the cold nights.

The same shit is still going down –
May spinning out
about her gear,
Jess coughing endlessly,
Joe storms out

and Frank – god what is it with him?
He has talked *all* day,
some of it's almost interesting.
I tried to answer hours ago
but gave up.
Something he took
has him wound up.

We're happy to be here
when we're not paranoid
or tripping or too stoned
to care.

The fire dies to nothing
and ash blows through the room.

It's lonely without furniture
might get some from the Salvos,
and it will
feel more
like home.

Yellow Glen

Joe flogged a box of Yellow Glen
and we had a party.

He is great at flogging stuff,
knows how to get around them.
When the blokes from the truck
wheel the trolleys into the shop
the 'watcher' – they always have a watcher now –
stays with the truck.

Joe has a different plan
each time.
Today he lit a fire against the wall
just near the truck,
worked a treat
and he got a box.

Jess is down.
Frank thinks she's pregnant,
wonders if she will
wear out her welcome
at the clinics.

Joe and May get pissed on one bottle,
laugh so much
they cry –
tell us after
they had some gear
they didn't share.

The night is warm.
Jess sings for us
and May starts to cry,
again.

Gone

I bombed out of school
after Mum died.
Lived with Grandad,
and wandered the streets.

I tried to stay –
Grandad tried to keep me there
but I felt my eyes glaze over in class,
my mind closed.
Year seven kids had a dare going,
asking me what it was like
to see a dead person.
Their frightened baby faces,
avoided my eyes.

Girls in short uniforms;
their backs to me.
I'd hear them talk
in whispers –
His dad killed his mum.

It was easier to hide
find a crowd where no one knew me.

So I changed my name
and
disappeared.

Floating

Warm Melbourne night
room full of some mob –
never seen them before,
floating away
on some good shit.

Tomorrow I'll work it all out.

Heatwave

Pulled from bed
by heat pouring through the wall,
my head pounding.

Outside trees, people, houses
all pale in the hot light.

The bike out the back that Joe stole
bursts its tyres
as heaviness presses into the city.
I go out, nothing better to do.

Ambulances cry up and down the streets,
the paper says people have died.

Neighbourhood

At the end of the road
streams of cars
flow on a hot grey river.

I hear their hum each day
one direction in the morning
the other in the afternoon.
It's so boring.

Condemned

There was a sticker
on the door:
'Stay out – Danger – For demolition'
There was a date too,
so we pulled the sign down,
chucked it away.

But the place is working well for us;
'West End Smash Repairs' one side,
empty factory the other.
A lovely spot in West Melbourne,
Stanley St, if you must know
but we are keeping our heads down
not advertising it.

Jess's Dream

Jess's been sick for weeks.
At night, when she goes to sleep
on the mattress in the corner,
we hear her dreams.

'They're running dreams,'
she tells us in the morning,
'I'm running all night,
it's night in the dream too.
Behind me are animals,
horses, dogs – big dogs,
a centaur.
They don't make any noise
because their hooves are covered
in cloth,
like velvet,
purple velvet.'

We sit around her
on the filthy mattress.
Frank has thrown out one lot of sheets,
but the next lot he got
weren't much better.
Why do people
give away stained sheets?

I can see one flower in the pattern
of climbing roses and leaves
that isn't stained.
I look hard at it.
It's pink,
a colour I'd forgotten.

Jess says the animals
can talk,
and they call her.
She can't remember what they say,
but they frighten her.

Sometimes she flies
in her dreams
but when she does
she has to be careful of the powerlines
that cross the city air
like laser beams
waiting to get her.

She gets trapped under the powerlines
with the animals
coming,

and she says
in the dream
her legs vanish
and she has to slide
along the footpath,
through the piss and the vomit
and she knows it's only
a matter of time
before
they catch up.

Chalk drawings

There's a guy,
does drawings down
on Swanston Street.
Went to Art School,
hung with the wrong crowd
got on the hard stuff.
We're all glad though,
his drawings
brighten our dull streets.

But today
he drew
a staircase that went down
into blackness.
It looked so real
I wanted to follow it.

May

May comes in late
eyes like red lamps.
We watch her
wary –
we know what's coming.
WHO THE FUCK HAS MOVED MY STUFF?
She yells and screams and throws things,
most of it hers.
We stand back.

May is tiny
dark
beautiful
cuts up her arms
throws up in the toilet
eats chocolate
fucks for money.

She speaks three languages
topped science at school
got her HSC on speed.

May rings her mum
hangs up before she answers
cries herself to sleep.

St Kilda Pier

Frank thinks he's the boss
of Jess
just because he's fucking her
and he thinks it's his baby,

thinks he's the boss of everyone.
He says, 'Today we are going to the sea.'
All grand like that
like we'll all just leap up
and get our buckets and spades.

Joe says, 'Fuck you! I'm staying here.'
'You busy?' Frank asks, smirking.
'Always busy you prick.'

May says she'll go
but the train cops know her
and all of us –
so we walk, Joe too.
Jess stumbles in her black and shiny
second-hand high heels.
Frank's protective
all over her.

Too tired to walk now
and it's miles from here
so we find a tram
and Jess sleeps on a seat.
People frown,

old ladies look at Jess
her heels, her legs.
Men look too, someone tuts.

Jess throws up
so we all get off at the next stop.
and laugh all the way down
St Kilda Pier.

Grandad calls

Grandad rings me.
'Hey Josh?'
'Mal,' I correct him,
'How'd you get this number?'

'Oh, Mal, look I tried a couple
of old ones –
on the off-chance, how are you?'
'Grandad you don't want to know.'
'Yes I do.'
'No you don't.'
'For God's sake Josh!'

'Mal.'
'Mal, please let me come and get you.
Take you out for tea or something –
we could talk.'

And then I feel bad.
'Sorry Grandad,' I say
'That's ok,' he says
'Maybe next week Grandad.'
'Ok,' he sighs, 'maybe next week.
But I'm going to keep trying ok?'

Modelling

Jess did some modelling
for this bloke.
Got paid a bomb.
You can imagine the type.
He wanted her to strip off.

She's in books now.
Her body wrapped
in a white net
as she walks naked
through water
– like she's already dead.

Joe

Joe has this way of sitting on the couch.
He burrows into it like it's made for him
and we all give way to him, move for him,
make room.

He reminds me of a friend's cat
back when I was growing up.
It ate birds and lizards,
left feathers and chewed guts
on the back door mat.

The family didn't seem to notice
because it was their friend.
He'd come in at night
after hunting and killing,
and they'd get up off seats
and let him sleep.

Kookaburra

In the middle
of the city
today,
I'm sure
I heard
a kookaburra
laughing.

Eavesdropping

A woman gets on the train.
She's dragging a large purple case.
She could be going to the airport,
but everyone knows she's not.
Her clothes for one,
then there's the scars up and down her arms,
the tatts,
and the smell of course.

She sees me and nods.
We don't make a big deal of seeing each other.

Then Raylene gets on.
'Fuck!' I breathe,
and slide lower in the seat.
She is loud and she sees me.

'Hi Mal! How's Jess?
Heard she was sick.
That girl needs get herself sorted!'
'Yeah sure,' I say, shut the fuck up, I think.
Then she sees the woman with purple suitcase.

'Hi Josie, you ok?'
She speaks even louder,
so the whole train carriage can hear.
'You on the move?'
She thinks it's her lounge room.

'I'm fine, what about you, you safe?'
I feel the train carriage lean towards them,
to hear how Raylene is.

Raylene is half cut.
She doesn't hide the bruised purple marks
that litter her arms.
She's too skinny.

'Yeah', she yells, 'I'm fuck'n fine,
but my shit boyfriend isn't,
I'm gonna kill him,
when I find him! Bastard!'
The train carriage is practicing active listening,
enjoying a bit of drama for the trip home,
happy, so long as it's not their life.

But some shift in their seats,
necks straining to check if it's their station;
keen to be gone.

'What's he done now?' Josie asks, adding fuel.
'Fuck'n lied about sleeping with some bitch,
beat me up and took my gear!'
Josie is making sympathetic noises.

My head is down.
iPod turned up
and I get off at the next stop,
some station I've never heard of.

Chapter 2

Memory loss | February

The young Jess

'It was a rich kid's school,'
she told me.
'We had everything,
then my parents split up.
Mum and I moved
and I watched that door close.'

I sat and listened to her.
She was beautiful,
she smelt amazing.
Some days I could barely breathe
when I saw her.

Jess spun into my world
into my grey state school
with all the brightness of clean air.
She spoke, and everyone took notice
they listened.

This was the young Jess –
the well Jess.

During English

We're doing *Merchant of Venice*,
out the front acting – Jess was Portia.
me – of course Bassanio, Portia's true love.
My fate is interrupted, as always.
'Josh? You're needed at the front office'
I leave the room,
and watch the teacher
hand my part to someone else.
Jess watches me go,
and I trip on the desk by the door.

I thought about just taking off,
but I see it's Mum
and Grandad at the office,
god what now?
'Mum! I haven't done anything honest. What's wrong?'
'We thought we should tell you,
we've spoken to the Head,
your dad's come home –
he's there now, we just have to try and help him make this work.'
'Are you for real?' I yell this loudly.
The ladies on the front desk look up from their typing.
Mr Gallagher comes out, 'Josh? You alright there mate?'
As I walk away, I hear him say
'We're trying to support him as much as possible...'
They're all so full of shit.

What the body remembers

Jess joins me on the oval
'You ok?'
'Yeah.'
'I heard about your dad, shit hey?
You wanna a smoke?'
'Yeah.'
'It's not that bad really, is it?' she's looking for smokes,
'Wanna bet?'

Then she pushes me over, laughing
and for a moment she's in my arms
laying in the grass,
my heart pounding against her
my lips in her hair.

She pulls herself up
looks at me still laughing,
and that was it,
never mentioned again.

But the shape of her had pushed
against me
and my body remembered.

Homecomings

I don't cry,
but last time he came home I did.
He hit me with his belt,
told me I needed to toughen up,
which I did.

He said that's how small blokes got by.
I always saw him as tall,
thought he was having a go at me.

Background pattern

I remember being young
and the smell of clean sheets
as Mum made the top sheet float
over me like a great white cloud.

Knowing that the key was kept
under the dead pot plant
by the back door,
and feeling grown up about it.
Taking phone messages for Mum
so she'd come home to them;
'Ring Fil bak,' written along the top of the newspaper
in blue crayon.
And later,
sneaking out at night
through my bedroom window,
thinking Mum never knew.

Fighting with her over Dad,
over secrets in our life,
over sadness.

I remember being young,
but the details are fading
into the background.

Like waking
and watching
a dream as it disappears.

Counsel

The school counsellor tells me
'Write down your dreams.'

The silence gets too loud
so I say,
'What if someone reads them?'

But he says,
'Does that really matter?'

Long division

At school
long division
is a mystery to me.
The numbers
move on the board,
my mind a blank.
Outside the sunbaked
bitumen smells like hot metal
and in the air
is a buzz of flies
throwing themselves
at the window.

A drama saves me from
one of these
long division days,
when the year nine kids
set fire to the toilets
and the teachers send us home,
with stern warnings and threats of police.

Jess and I catch the train
into town,
hang out at Flinders Street Station,
stirring up the homeless bums
on the steps,
laughing as we pick out
dealers in the crowd.

We are idiots,
running blindly
into fire.

Best friends

May was always Jess's best friend.
Girls together forever! written on their schoolbooks.

They'd dress up,
put on Jess's mum's makeup,
smudged thick on their faces.

Jess moved to my school
when her mum moved out.
May stayed at the posh school.

'I hate my mum!' she told me
sitting on the oval smoking.
'She made me come to this crap school.'
'Gee thanks,' I sulked.

Jess laughed then
leant forward,
her long fingers
just touching
the hairs on my arm.
'Not you, you duffer,
I love you.'

She used words
like love and hate
too freely
back then.

Up north

Mum told me Dad was up north.
'Why?' I'd hassle her.
'Because that's where he works,
he'll be home in a few months.'
Mum has a streak of grey hair
that runs from her hairline
over her left eye,
down through her hair.
Her forehead creases up as she talks,
and I know something is wrong.

Then he's home –
and I think,
this isn't my dad
I'd ask her over and over.
'Who's taken my dad?'

The lie cracked open one day
and I found out about prison,
about him never even leaving Melbourne –
learnt the hard way
about the grievous bodily harm.

And as he came roaring back through our door
I wondered who was meant to save us.
Why was no one protecting us from him,
why he was my dad,

and why it was ok
for a stranger to live in our house
beating up on us?

And the picture of my real dad
living up north
in the warmth,
just wouldn't go away.

Trauma

Now it's late.
I can hear my dad
prowl the house
like a lion.
I hide,
but my mum
can't stay out of his way
she's his prey,
and he will come for her
when he's good and ready.

The loud bloke

My dad hangs on every corner,
he's every bastard I see,
everyone who tries to take me down.

In the pub, he's the loud bloke,
the 'she'll be right!' bloke.
The bloke who reckons
he never has too much to drink
and is never out too late.
But when he's home, it's always
too often
for his wife and kid.

Prison prose

I was twelve, three years before he came back for the last time, when I found out that Dad wasn't up north. The phone rang, Mum was out the back and she called for me to answer it. It was this bloke, he said he was a mate of Dad's and could he talk to him?

I said Dad was away working up north. 'Working? Is that what they call it now?' and the bloke on the other end just start laughing. 'Call what?' I asked but I already had a bad feeling about it. 'He's probably in prison again you little prick, your mother's busy trying to keep it quiet but you need to know because you'll end up in there too!' he hung up still laughing. I don't know how long I stood there in the blue air listening to the empty phone beep at me. Mum was watering a small patch of garden she'd planted with orange and purple flowers. The bright petals hung down under the weight of the water. I hated the bastard at the end of the phone for telling me, but I hated Mum for not telling me.

Cake

When I'm alone
I think about Mum,
and how when I was little
she would bake cakes.

I'd watch her
mix the sugar and butter,
add the eggs, the flour,
then she'd say
'Josh, what flavour do you want today?'
I would have already decided because
I knew she would ask,
mostly I wanted lemon.

Today I want chocolate.
I want clean out the bowl.
I want to hear her voice,
talking away to me
as she cleans up.
I want to wait for the smell rising from the oven,
listen for the timer,
feel the heat of the kitchen,

but more than anything
I want Mum to be alive.

Eskimo

Grandad's part Eskimo.
Well that's what he told me.
'That's why your mum and you
have beautiful eyes.'

I was little when he told me this,
and I was impressed.
This was before
I hated my eyes
for making me a target.

He told me stories
as I sat on the bench in his shed,
watching him work away
at fixing Mum's broken chair.

He told long stories about
an ancestor
who went to Canada
in search of gold,
but found a woman
with soft curving eyes.

'And that's were you came from.'
He'd say this looking up at me,
like it should all make sense,
like he's showing me those eyes.

This story of his great, great grandfather
and the Eskimo woman
rests in my brain,
it's filed away with childhood stories
of magic
and make-believe.

History lesson

Jess was the first one
to take ecstasy.
The first one to shoot up.

She was running
and wouldn't stop.

'Hey Mal, let's run away'
she said one night, eyes glazed,
I almost got my hopes up,
that it was me she wanted.
But no, she was running.

The day she found May
again,
she said it was karma.
'This is meant to be,
us three together.'

We were fourteen
and should have been home.

But we took speed,
a drank a bottle of Vickers,
and talked nonstop
until
morning.

Remember

I remember my home,
clean clothes.
I remember being warm.
I remember Dad coming home.
I remember once
seeing them hug.

I remember screaming,
the smell of burning.
I remember flashing blue lights
filling my room bright as lightning.
I remember neighbours across the street,
arms folded tight across dressing gowns.
I remember rain,
haloes around street lights.
I remember being cold,

I can't remember what happened to Mum.

The mountains

Once Grandad took me to the mountains.
We stayed in a cabin
with a floor that moved
as we walked.
It rained most of the time
and all our clothes got
soaked on the first day.

After we'd been stuck inside for days
we went down to the cliff.
From there the water fell for miles
into the green forest below.

I could feel myself
flying through the air
with the water,
falling,
falling.
I watched one drop
as it got lost in the trees
and the mist.

In the afternoons
while he had a sleep,
I'd nick off into the rain
and smoke down by the toilet blocks.

One night we went out to the pictures.
I don't remember the movie,
but I remember Grandad cried.

I think he was trying to make life normal
but I was already too angry
for that.

School counsellor

He says,
'It's going to be hard for a while.'
I squirm in my seat.
'Are you laughing at me?'

He tries to keep me talking
but I don't say anything.
The silence shines around me
like armour,
my ears ring
like screaming.

Best keep my thoughts to myself.
I'd sound mad if I said them aloud.

Chapter 3

Speed | March

Speed

Thursdays are good.
May usually scores,
blows her pension and more
up her arms –
stops her in her tracks.

I'm interested in something
faster
to take away
the minutes and hours.

My small tablets
can take whole days away.

The life around me lightens
as I fold time
and escape.

Father dream

I

I wait for the door to open.
A key
is being turned
chains rattle,
a man coughs.

I'm aware of many men.
Warm bodies.
Someone coughing,
I have to step over them
to get to the end of the room.
The smell
like fur and dirt.

At the end of the room
I see my reason for coming
and remember.

He is tall
arms hang at his side.
Legs apart, knees bent
like he's ready to run –
again.

Soon I'll get to him
over this river of people.
The room is hot
then cold.

The moon shines behind him,
and shadows
fall across his eyes
in black pools.
Dark lines run down
where his mouth and nose should be.
He is yelling, pieces of white spit
fly out of his mouth.

II
I wake –
I always wake
just before I reach him.

The smell is me,
foul and unwashed.
The shouting is me too
and Frank yelling at me
to 'shut the fuck up!'

The moon isn't here,
he's not here.

The crowd of people in the dream
are my friends,
but they frighten me too.
Awake or asleep
the fear is the same.

Secondhand

I got a woollen overcoat
from Jess.
She found it somewhere.
What I sleep in
what I wear –
all given
or stolen –

the Xbox, iPod
and the telly
and the light
and the table
I could go on – but you get the picture.

It was the same at home
with Mum –
nothing new.
'New stuff doesn't matter'
she'd say,
but it would be nice.

Real life

I'm writing this down
so you know.
You think everyone knows,

but they don't.
What they know are clichés;
small folds of my life
like taken from a newspaper,
not my real life.

Coco's

May loves to dance
and drags me out
to Coco's on Swanston Street.
We climb the six flights of dank stairs
to the soft air of the roof top bar.

Because there's a view
we think the air is clean
and take such deep breaths
that we send our heads spinning
and giggle at each other –
silly before the first drink.

May takes her skinny form
to the centre of the dance floor
moving away from me
into her own world.
Her light dress falls about her.
All eyes turn to look
as she winds herself through sound.

I wait for her,
but she only seems to wake
and look for me
when the music stops.

Old George

The Burke Street Mall moves in a mass
of shoppers
but I still find George
sitting alone on a bench
out the front of David Jones.
He's eyeing off
perfect women at the counters
trying on makeup.

'Hey you,' he says at me,
his methadone smile
empty of teeth.

He's alone for many reasons,
one is that he stinks.

'Why sit here torturing yourself old George?'
he just shrugs.

He is ageless,
under the dirt
he might be thirty.
Looks twice that.

Ever the smartarse, he says
'I had to sit here,
last seat in the whole mall.'

George is a storyteller.
He likes to share
all the facts he ever heard.

'Did you know the average person
swallows a thousand spiders
in their lifetime?'

'The Irish language,' he continues,
'describes emotions
as if they were the weather:
The sadness falls upon me.'
he says to great effect
as if he were truly Irish.

'Where do you pick up all this rubbish?'
'Read it somewhere, to be sure!'

I like to sit with old George.
It passes the time,
and he makes me smile.

'Been a lot
of sadness and rain in Ireland.'
He says, his eyes on the slim legs
at the make up counter.

Always

When I'm here,
I want to be somewhere else.

Always
looking for the next thing.

The next thought,
next action.

Playing it all out before it comes
so when it does
I know just what to do.

But I'm tired before I start,
and disappointed at the end.

It's never like I thought.

Party agenda

Our place
is one room.

May has a mob
here for a party,

some prick
has gone
through
my stuff,

someone
is throwing up,

someone is crying,
there's a fight
in the street

and the cops will
be here soon.

Black bears

George tells me about black bears.
His facts are sketchy
but it's a good story.

'They live in the high country,
the sky there is huge
and travels on to where the world ends,
air so fresh
the animals are all high.'

'Yeah right,' I say.
George told me last week
a koala lives in the Botanical Gardens
so I just nod.

We are in the Fitzroy Gardens
taking in the day,
sun playing at the leaves and
the grass like a great green cushion.

'The female black bear,' he goes on
marks her territory,
leaves her scent
on tree trunks.
The smell lets the males know
what mood she's in.'

'Bullshit!
That's scary George.'

'Yeah, but I reckon
it makes life easier
for the blokes.'

Frank

Frank has a devil in his brain.
Even when he's straight, he's mad –

like he made some deal
and gave his soul away
for a laugh.

He pushes us around,
hurts Jess,
then says he's sorry.

I don't know why we let him stay.
He's like a tomcat
we can't get rid of.

Joe ignores him,
baits him, fights him,
May and I avoid him,
and Jess sleeps with him –
it's totally gross.
He's twenty-four
too old for us.
– our resident drug supply.

He has a dark frown
that he wears
like a tattoo.
I don't think he has
a smile.

Centrelink

We go to Centrelink
to sort out our fortnightly cheque.
It reminds us what the government is for:
to employ dickheads.

Frank calls it our bank.
'Just off to see the bank manager.'
he tells the bloke at the 7-Eleven.
'oh...ok,' the bloke, as intelligent as ever.

I feel like I'm waiting for drugs to dull my brain,
but they just seem to be making everyone else stupider.

Frank is sparky today
almost happy, so I'm suspicious.
He's never happy.
Jess doesn't know what's up,
and she's too sick to care.
He drags her everywhere
'Leave her home,' I say,
but he ignores me.
She doesn't seem to be able to say no to him.

We take a number and sit down.
Melissa is my 'Centrelink Officer' today.
She's about twenty,
all dressed up, a ton of makeup
but she knows fuck all about the job.
Her supervisor hovers nearby.

'How many job interviews or enquires have you had this week?'
Melissa's reading from a sheet of paper.
'None.' I say.
'Ok, you know we'll have to stop your payments
if you don't look for work in the next two weeks.'

'Listen, I'm on a pension, not Newstart,
I don't have to be looking for work.
Have you looked at my file? What does it say?'
I start to turn the computer screen around.

Melissa stands up in alarm and others come running.

'If you cut off my money, I'll come looking for you.'
I speak low and menacing
like in the movies, then storm out for effect.

Later I moan to George about it.
'If I was rich, they wouldn't treat me like that.'
'If you was rich, you wouldn't have to go there,
you dickhead.'

Oh yeah,
maybe the drugs are working.

Journal

I get out my journal.
It's hidden in the side pocket
of my pack.
No one knows it's there.
They know I write in it though.

Jess had a go the other day.
'Give us a read.'
'I would,' I said, making a joke,
'but I would have to kill you after.'
It wasn't far from the truth.

I read a line I can't remember writing,
Each breath crushes me.

Maybe I should visit
a counsellor again
like I did when I was at school,
but then I would have to speak.
I can't say the words out loud,
not yet.
Only write them here,
and hide them away.

From the street

A boy wearing so many chains on his black pants
he holds them up with one hand
 as he hurries to keep up with his mates.

A woman whose face hangs down on one side,
and when she smiles at me,
her whole mouth moves around to the left.

A girl on her mobile phone:
'You always have options,' and,
'No, I'm not going to, not ever,' and,
'It's just a number, it doesn't say anything about you.'
I wish this girl could be my friend.

A guy on his mobile phone:
'I'm going to start eating tomorrow,' and,
'Yeah, I'm in detox', and,
'Yeah, thanks, as long as I can tick the boxes.'
I don't want another friend like this.

A tribe of tiny grey swans
circling in brown water.
The sparrows outside Melbourne Central,
trigger the automatic doors
and fly inside.

The bloke who gives people rides
in his horse and cart
along Swanston Street,

yells at his kids.
'Piss off back to your mother,
I've got work to do!'
I look to where he points
and there's young woman at a café,
a baby on her knee,
and another in a pram.

An old lady plays piano
further along the street,
so hunched over her keyboard,
her long ragged hair
covers her hands.
An evil eye protects her
and she plays like you wouldn't believe.

Grandad's visit

'Hey Mal? There's some old bloke here,
says he's your grandad.'
Joe shrugs at me
flops back on the couch.

I lead him away from our place
to a café down the road.
He buys the coffee.
'How did you find me?

'Oh, I asked around.'
'Did you tell the cops?'
'No – no I didn't.'

He looks tired,
old age cuts deep
but his eyes are the same,
warm and bright
like Mum's.

'You look like shit,' he's saying,
why don't you come home?
You'll get sick.'
'I'm fine,' I lie, 'I'm good.'

'I can get you into rehab.'

'Grandad, don't try and find me again.'

I get up and walk away,
trying to stop the sudden sob –
like a needle in my chest.

Stomach pain

I'm eating,
first time in days.
May is eating again too.
'Food is only important
when there isn't any,' she says,
stuffing pieces of stolen chicken in her mouth –
like she's wise.
And we laugh until our stomachs ache.

Purple dust

Wind rolls like purple dust
down Collins Street.
I'm here because of May.
She told me I could get lemon gelato for $1 cup.
She knows it's my favourite.

Down the hill,
overdressed theatre-goers
teeter on the edge of the pavement
out of practice in their high heels.
Another new show has cycled into town
like the speed of Melbourne's seasons.

Us city scum watch Pricilla and Abba lovers
mimic their heroes,
making drag queens an everyday thing.

Sequined dresses stretch over bulges.
They drink pink daiquiris
and think they look clever.

The last of gelato is bitter
on my tongue,
as the pink crowd disappear
up the stairs.

And pieces of fake purple feather boa
and ruby red sequins
glitter in the gutters.

The library

If I dress nice,
put on Joe's aftershave,
I can sit in the old library,
where the glass dome roof
lifts into the sky.

I look interested in the books,
try not to look at the people.
I smell the light, the air
thick with words, the stories
roll into my head,
even when my eyes are closed.

The dusty light is strained
through a hundred years
of history.

Letters and quotes
float about and
the silence
rings with voices.

Malcolm

My mum called me Josh.
That was years ago.
I was just a kid.

One night a bloke called me
Malcolm
and it stuck.

Broken English

There is blaring noise,
cascading car crashes,
and rifle fire.

Bobby sits encased
in a red plastic car.
'Fuck! Fucking hell!'
he yells at his virtual world.

I say 'Hey you,'
and he pulls up quick,
like he's used to trouble.

His eyes slowly clear,
his fighting arm relaxes.
'Fuck bro, you make me jump!
what your name 'gen?'
'Mal,' I say smiling.

I remember
the years of him,
sitting up the back of class
because he was just too much trouble,
the fractured language pouring from him
like a beacon
for every bastard to try and stomp out.

We shake hands – street style.
Old bros from way back.

'What the fuck you doin' now?'
'What about you?' I dodge his question.
'Live rough, hey, on the streets, you know?'

He looks bad,
his drug-soaked words blur,
and his eyes run red,
with a twisted old man smile.

'Fuck Bobby,'
what else is there to say?
He looks worse than me.

The zoo

When you're stoned
it's always good to find something to do.
Makes the gear last longer,
and you don't feel so bad
coming down.

Jess and I get the train
to Royal Park.
George calls this,
'Knowing your environment.'
He reckons we should find
a new place every week.
'Keeps you thinking,' he says.
'Makes you think
you're thinking,' I say back,
quoting someone.

Cost us a fortune to get in
so we have to see everything.

In the butterfly house,
dusty wings settle on Jess.
Colours bright
and hazy.
We sit on the boardwalk
in the humid air,
stay for ages.

The people at the zoo
make us laugh
more than the animals.
Some people are so fat
we can't see what's in the cages.

The gorilla reminds us of someone,
then we realise it's George,
and fall over laughing.

Jess is too tired to keep going
so we lie in the shade
eating ice creams
and watch the children on the carousel.

In the train on the way home
Jess holds my hand.
We are like an old couple,
who know they can never be together.

Bobby

I see Bobby
in the street again

'Hey bro, small world.'
He smiles,
knows who I am now.

He's all blue and puffy
around his eyes.
'What's up?' I say.
'Cops,' he says.
'Shit.'
'Yah.'
'Bastards.'

Work

Frank has a job.
You could have knocked me over
with a cone.
'Where?' Joe asks.
'Bullshit,' says May,
and so on.
Disbelief is the general response.

'Thanks a lot you bastards!'
Frank heads for the door,
the usual storming off,
but Jess stops him.
'Tell us,' she says.

'Up Swanston Street,
you know, the café opposite RMIT.'
'Crap! no one would employ you.
You stink, your clothes, face, your arms
are fucked – on yeah and your head!'
Joe's harsh sometimes,
but he has a point.

'Look, you fuckwit, I've got a job,
I need to try something different.'

'What? How long before they find out
you're pinchin' the biscuits!'
'As if I'd do that!'
'Right!'

Frank jumps Joe.
Jess lies down and goes to sleep.
May walks out,
and I turn the telly on, loud.

Home improvements

After the door
was smashed in
Joe put up a piece of tin,
but it shakes in the night
rattling against the wind,
and I hear people arriving
who aren't there.

May's story

'At the end of year twelve,
I found out I was pregnant.'
She tells me this,
when she's drunk.

'It was too late to get rid of it,
and too late to hide it
from my parents.

They arranged a marriage –
strict India business.
"Oh the shame of it!"
but I couldn't marry a man I hated.
"I'm too young,"
so they sent me away.'

I try to picture May pregnant,
her stomach round, but I can't.
It reminds me too much of Mum and the baby
that was there one day and gone the next.

May's baby was taken.
He was twelve hours old.

You're young, the nurses told me,
You'll bounce back,
But I found heroin,
that men liked my body,
my dark skin.

My belly was flat again,
my breasts empty.
Too quickly, there was nothing
of my little boy.'

Her boy is in foster care.
'He could be anywhere'
She's crying now.
'Fuck don't cry May.'
I try and help
but I just make it worse.

La Bohème

Jess got a ticket to the opera from a punter.
After she'd done what he'd wanted
he handed her this ticket.
She told him she wanted cash
but he insisted,
said she'd enjoy herself.

So she dresses up
and when she's ready
we all hold our breath.
'Shit Jess,' Frank says.
She looks thirty
and like she really
knows what she's about.

We take a tram
May does Jess's face.

We leave her at the Arts Centre,
and as we go, she's smiling.
We bum around in front of the rowing sheds
down by the Yarra, waiting,
and throw rubbish in the water
to keep from getting cold.

We see her at ten-thirty,
her face glowing.

It's like she's been in prison
and tonight she's free.

She cries as she tells us the story,
about the lovers who can't be together.
She sings part of a song she remembers.

And in the dark by the river,
with the city lights snaking over the water,
we hear her voice
strong and true
again.

Sleep

Joe takes off for hours –
whole days sometimes,
and we think he is lost.

But he always comes back,
bruised and sorry looking,
still fine about life.
He dumps another
pile of stolen junk in front of us.

He falls onto the couch,
too tired to talk,
pushing his shape
into the cushions
and sleeps.

Coffee

I have enough money
for a coffee
so, I sit at a café
like I'm doing things
regular.

The waiter looks at me
I smile.
He is tall and dark.
Italian I think.
He doesn't smile.

I remember then how I look,
that I'm just visiting
this world
that streams into the city each day
pouring from trains,
tight with bodies.

I read the paper,
someone has won an award,
the war continues,
in Iraq, the cricket, the tennis.
Can't read for long;
I'm out of practice.

The manager
comes out anyway,
moves me on.

This thing they do

May and Jess have
this thing they do.
They dress up the same,
same clothes,
same jewelry,
and they go out.

They look frightening,
too beautiful,
different yet the same.
Men can't help but stare.
I tell them I can't protect them.
I'm just their tough little friend.

They tell me they do it for a laugh.
One small and dark,
the other tall and blonde.
But they could be sisters.

Working the crowd

My mate Carlos's begging
at Melbourne Central.

Back up on Swanson Street,
there's a protest on because
Israel is bombing the crap
out of the West Bank.

Carlos couldn't give a shit.
The protest crowd isn't good for money
so, he's downstairs working the station mob.

Today his line is
he and his missus
need forty-two bucks to stay at the Salvos.
For good measure, he adds that she's pregnant.

The station is a good place to work.
He can go up and back
without asking the same person twice.

Trains go every six minutes
so he has hundreds of people
he can approach at peak hour.

He knows he'll get more if he's polite,
says 'excuse me'
and only looks a little disappointed
when they say no.

Knows about body language too.
Keeps his hands out of his pockets,
patiently explains the situation.
Shrugs his shoulders,
doesn't push people.

He's a true artist.

He has to stick to the same story
so that people aren't on to him.
Always asks women
or men who are with women.
Never groups of men.
Crowded stations are good,
empty stations are bad news.

He tells me this late one night.
He's stoned
on the shit he bought
with the two hundred bucks
he got today.

Says he's thinking of writing
it all down.
Thinks he's got something
to teach kids.

Jess's drawing book

She draws faces –
blackened eyes
cheeks streaked
with red
hair streaming
in the still wind.

Tripping

In the dark I can feel them,
people quietly breathing.
They're soft,
I think I can trust them,
No one touches me, gets in my way.
They move aside if I come too close.
They're my friends.

We don't talk.
We just walk.
I think I'm dead,
and it's ok.
The light fades slowly,
moves away,
going somewhere else.
The darkness moves into the space
where the light has left.
My eyes change, dilate,
I can see everyone.
Maybe I'm dreaming.

I'm tired now,
but it's good to walk.
I walk by someone, so close I hear her sigh.

They move slowly,
no air moves.

Someone is standing still in the blackness,
their shape shimmers into form.
I'm not afraid to walk by,
no need to speak.
They're my friends.

Light sneaks in cracks,
runs along in bright lines
but I turn my back
and go deeper into the dark.
Blackness folds in on me,
warmth like an embrace holds me.

The pain has faded here
 in the black space.

I reach out, touch someone,
they touch me,
they kiss me.
I move to the next person, they take me in the dark.
A man in a suit touches my body,
I move past him
the suit smells old.

I hear a sigh next to me.
Rough hands.
More than
one person.
It is a woman,

two women,
one whispers
'Why don't you come with us?'
Light seems to pour in with her words.

I am in pain,
alive not dead.
I can feel burning,

The crystal spell cracks
and breaks.

Falling

Stoned too early.
I think its loneliness.

Out on the game,
I ended up in a place I don't know.

The wrong side of town
freaks me.

I'm losing my touch
for this.

My cornered friend

When I come home,
I call out so they know it's me
and not the cops
or some other losers.
Today no one answers
so I figure the place is empty.

I'm knocking around
making noodles on the camping stove
when I hear something at the back of the room,

and I find Joe lying in the corner,
behind the couch he usually claims.

He is breathing loudly,
his eyes darting about the place.

'Joe, what's up?'
I look him over.
Can't find anything straight off.
'I'm staying here,' he says,
'I'm not confessing.'
This Joe is freaking me out.
I like the fearless one better.

There's blood on his sleeve.
'Shit Joe, what's going on?'
'I didn't mean to.'
'You blood idiot, you've killed someone!'

'No! God no! She's not dead, she's fine.
I had to leave!'

'Joe, you're not making sense.'

'We'd taken something,
it was good shit.
We were getting into it
when someone came in,
started throwing stuff around.
They had a knife.
They got her and I ran.'

And I watch as Joe cries.
The bullshit artist, the 'man'
the loner.
'She might die Mal,'
my cornered friend sobs.

Joe's friend

'Stabbing victim found in abandoned factory.'
The headlines tell the story.
Joe stays hidden,
thinking they're coming
for him.

Ugly is the new black

There are so many of us now,
we make the city ugly.
I know when it happens,
when I become ugly,
because eyes slip over me
and I'm invisible.

Living like this
I grow more ugly,
more invisible.
The face I had
is gone –
and I have changed
into
someone else.

Jess turns seventeen

Jess celebrated
her seventeenth birthday
in a brothel.

Earned a thousand bucks.
We go out to a club
but the drinks
get stuck
in my throat.

The devil

I have a shadow in my eye
that moves
away into darkness
when I turn.

It hides,
sulks when I pretend
it's not there.

Old George calls it
the devil –
says he's got one too.

Chapter 4

Into the dark | June

The knife

I'm walking down a back lane
after ten on a Monday.
The Suits have gone
and the city is ours.
The walls are all coloured here
wild and lurid
as if my stoned brain
is splattered on the bricks.
A tram lurches down Flinders Street,
blurs its way along
like a moving fluoro light.

Edgy now for the gear,
I wait for Joe
and I check dark spaces –
those fuck'n doorways
have freaked me out since I was a kid.

A shadow of black
moves to my left.
'Joe?'
I turn
but it's not Joe.
He gets me below the ribs.
A fist hard as a rock takes all my air.

I turn back fast
finding breath,
my knife ready.

It is a fact of life –
I hate him
he hates me.

I make like I'm punching
but the knife cuts deep.
He's standing closer than I thought
air push out of him
as he goes down.

I take off at a run
'round the corner
and disappear in the darkness.

Raid

Got raided yesterday.
Plain-clothed cops
knocked the door down
like heroes.
I hid up the lane until they were gone.
The pricks!
Looking for 'illicit substances', they said,
Rubber gloved
they pulled everything apart,
left us with more mess than ever
in our shit world.

Writing of love

Ok, so I don't do this,
but since you asked,
I'll try and explain.

I have *attachment* issues
(I've been told),
so I don't fall in love
as a rule,
until I met Flora.

She was funny,
reminded me of Jess
back when we were at school.

Flora was wearing black.
Black laddered tights,
black mini,
black top and makeup,
but her skin was translucent
pearly and glowing,
and she was stoned.

I was in a bar down a lane
and I had money,
which meant I had just done a job
or was about to score.

She was talking to a cop.
He stood out a mile with his shaved head
and clean look.

I could hear her laugh
in the still moments
between the music.

He was hitting on her
hard.
But she stood her ground.
I knew I had a chance,
she was talking to him
but looking straight
at me.

Talk into your ears

Her name was Flora
'Like the margarine,' she said
smiling.
But in the noise of the nightclub
I thought she said
'Laura'
and the reference to margarine
made no sense.

All that noise muffles sound.
People talk into your ears
like that will help.

Anyway Flora –
she was on to me
straight away
had me sewn up,
wanted me to meet the parents
before I'd caught her
second name.

'I don't know about this,'
I said on the tram
on the way past the old Pentridge.
'What would you tell them about me?'
 'You're a uni student
studying Law at RMIT?'

Laneways

Flora has money today
and we get a table
stepping around bags and feet.
'Lanes are not just for smackheads,'
she whispers at my ear.

At night this lane is empty.
Roller doors bright with graffiti
pulled shut,
and the stink of piss
flowers in damp corners.

Now in daylight, we watch
Japanese tourists pose
against painted walls,
the chaos of graffiti,
like our lives on display.
At the crowded Spanish café,
an Irish waitress takes our order.
The place buzzes with music and people
and the night stink
blends with smells of spice and coffee.

Jealousy

'Where did you find her?'
'Come on Jess – be nice.'
'She's a bitch Mal and you know it.'
'She's just a friend.'
'Right, what about us?'
Her lip curls out the question.
'Us?'
Now I'm surprised and can't hide it.
'Yes us. Aren't we mates? Her hands run up my arms,
stop at my shoulders.
She pulls me in close.
'And remember we said no one else can be here?
There's no room for *anyone* else.'
'She's not moving in.'
'But she's with you.'
'And you're with that fuckwit Frank.'
'I need him Mal.'
'To keep you supplied.'
'You're stronger than me.'
'Right,' I say pulling away.

Flora stands outside in the street, waiting,
I watch her light up another smoke.
'Look Jess, we'll have to talk about this later,
I have to go.'
'Ok, go!
There's nothing to talk about.'

Flora's out on the street,
she's got high boots on,
black stockings and a short skirt,
such great legs.
I want to go.
'Right, ok,' I say distracted.
'You are a bastard Mal.'
Jess turns her back on me.

Sex

There is no time
for talk.
We pull at clothes
We hurry –
not really sure why,
but if I close my eyes
I can be inside the passion,
inside the moment.
And she can be a goddess
that I'm fucking.

Flora in bed

'So, what's with that bitch?'
I'm still catching my breath
and she's on to the next thing,
lighting a joint.
'Jess?' I say gathering myself.
'Yeah, she's a bitch, saw that straight off.'
What is it with women? I lay back.
'Well?' she's leaning over me,
her breasts so fine in my face
and I really don't want to talk about Jess.
Flora can talk pretty much anytime.
'Com' on,' I say, 'let's talk later.'

The thing is

'The thing is,
I think you love her
and you're with me because she's rejected you.'

I'm over this and it shows.
'It's not important who I'm with,
or who she's with,
or who anyone's with.
It'll be over soon –
You'll shoot up too much shit,
I'll get into ice,
Frank'll meet a messy end some dark lane,
Joe'll end up in prison,
Jess'll get sicker,
May'll be sadder.
What does it matter?
I don't care if you're jealous or she is.
What does it matter?'

She slaps me hard,
which I deserved
but she did fuck me again
before she left.

The wind

On Thursday night
the wind
pulls hard.
Alone again, walking –
wet roads mirror flashing lights.

I step off the pavement
and see my reflection,
the building above me
pictured on the road
in hard lines of glass and concrete.

My face almost featureless,
made stranger
by drops and splashes of passing cars.
It's an old man I see,
hairline slipping back
eyebrows thickened to fill the space.

It's like a comic drawing of a face
– a joke.

More rain and the face becomes mine again,
the buildings focus,
lights flash again.

And the wind,
like the third person
in every thought,
demanding as a child,
pushes at me
to move on.

Flora

I fell into Flora
like a safety net
like a sweet dream
like a drug.

The look of her
her look of love
her open arms.
I thought I was safe.

Stoned together
we flew
far away from here.

I didn't see
the crash, didn't feel
the fall, didn't hear
the rushing in my ears.

I felt a lot of things
with her
one of them I thought
was love.

and when she left
I came down
cold turkey
cold as death.

Leaving

'Hey George
I'm going to leave,
thought I'd go on a holiday.'

George for once,
looks like he's listening.
'Ok,' he says.

'I'm going to the beach,
somewhere I can
sit and watch the sea.'

'Right,' says George.

'I don't even want
to swim,
it'd be too cold anyway.'

'Sure,' he says.

'George, are you listening to me?'
He looks at me vaguely.
'Nup,' he says,
'Didn't hear a word.'

St Vincent's

We take Jess to the hospital
on the hill in Victoria Parade.
In A&E we pace like expectant fathers.
'Are you family?' the nurse asks.
'No,' we have to say.
'I'm her boyfriend,' Frank tries,
but they push us out
into the waiting room.

The doctor wakes me hours later.
'We're admitting her, she's unconscious.'
'What's wrong with her?'
My eyes wouldn't focus.
The doctor looking blurred and distant,
has the hard face of a long-term Emergency worker–
knows too much just by looking.
'She's got hepatitis,
her kidneys are shot,
she's pregnant and we're testing her for STI's,
her arms are a mess and we can't find a decent vein.'
Your friend has septicaemia and is dangerously ill.'

He looks right at me,
for a moment all judgment falls away.
It only lasts a moment.
'You can see her at Visiting Time.'
and he's gone,
white coat flashing through swinging doors.

Frank is edgy.
'Time to go,' he says.
'What about Jess?
She's really sick you bastard!'
I lay into him right there
until Security throws us all out.

Hospital visit

In her restless sleep
she fights whole worlds
while I wait through the quiet night.

Her sleeping self
does the two-voice thing
only the question and the answer
are a babble of dreamtalk.

I'd help if I could
even wake her up
tell her I love her
but I don't.

I touch her burning arm
hoping her sleeping self will just know

But she flinches like I've hit her.

Cold

Winter falls cold
on our squat
and we
can't get
warm.

Escape

I'm out late, getting some gear for May.
It's dark but the cops see me.
I'm sure they do.
So I'm off,
tripping over tins,
falling over rubbish in the lane.
The blue and red lights
scream and flash
off the walls.
I think I hear my name.
'Little prick' someone says.
I go in a side door and up the stairs.
I know this place,
and from the roof I see them running
like black ants.

Message from another universe

The ice ghoul down the end of our lane
tells me the police are looking for me.
'You gotta get out of here man.'
His eyes flick past me
hands jitter restlessly
grabbing at his shirt buttons
for comfort.

I use to care about them
in the beginning.
Ice freaks scared me
into caring.
Now I walk past,
leave them to their dark world.
They roam
in a separate universe
lost to even junkies and dope heads.

He means well though
has good contacts,
and it's hard to tell
but he might even care.

A dream

People out the front of cafés,
smoking. I'm strangely happy.
Old Italian men at the café say
hello like we're old friends.
I turn mid stride to say hello back.

I smile as I walk.
I've got new white runners on –
they come down hard on the pavement,
echo as I pound along.

Jess sits at one of the tables,
which is both odd, and completely normal.
She has a smoke in her hand.
She's leaning her elbows on the table, looking around.
She looks good.
New clothes – white smile.

'Hi, Mal.'
Of course I go to her.
Jess is well again,
looking like her old self.
'Nice clothes,' I say,
'Isn't it great to be here?'
She looks happy.
I know something is wrong
but can't quite place it.

Jess is eating chocolate.
Maybe it's a Harry Potter thing,
where eating chocolate will help.
It seems to be working.

She frowns at me.
'That's a bad bruise.'
She runs her fingers over the black patch on my arm.
'I know, don't touch it, it hurts.'

We are being normal,
this is nice.
'You look good Jess,' I say
and she smiles.

But my phone rings.
'I have to go.'
'Why? I've got something I need to tell you,
I have just remembered something from years ago.
Please stay.'
'Ok,' I say, even though I want to go.
I don't want to hear her memory.
This is like a flying dream,
I have to concentrate hard to stay up in the air.

'Can you tell me later?'
'No Mal – I need to tell you now, then I have to go.'

Shit, this is a dream.

'Do you remember when we use to come into the city
when we pissed off from school?'

'Yeah,' I'm worrying now.
'What about it?'
but Jess is going see-through.
'Jess stay!'
The phone rings and rings,
I can't seem to answer it.

When I wake, I am crushed.
Jess is in hospital,
not having coffee somewhere.
The phone rings out.
I play back the message.
May's voice shaking.
'Mal, you have to come to the hospital.
It's Jess.'

Chapter 5

Punishment | July

Jess

Jess died
two days ago.
None of us were there.

Frank is long gone.
I was hiding from the cops,
so was Joe.
May was God knows where.

I still don't know
where her mum is.
If I did
how would I tell her?

Her body is in the morgue.
She is one of the stars
the city lights block out each night.

Winter

The sky closes in.
Midwinter, the cold
is a physical presence.
Thick cloud touches
the city
and just walking
we're drenched.
I'd quite like it
if I had
clothes to change into.
A place that was
warm.

Rain

Today it rained again.
Thick grey sheets fell for hours.
Tim's chalk drawings
ran down Burke Street
like a coloured river.

I got so wet
the smell rose off me
in steam.
I smelt like
wet dog
or something worse.
People turned looking for the smell
then gave me a wide berth.

I'm only young you know
but some days
I feel like I'm just treading water
waiting.
On dark days
I speed it up, take anything I can find.

I want the end.

Difficult

I find a bloke at the Salvos
I can talk to.
He found me really.
Came on all nice and friendly,
then tried to sort my life out.

But it's ok.
Passes the time.
When I've got nothing better to do
I go and hang around the Centre
hassle everyone
until Bob – the counsellor, comes out.

He knows I'm wired today.
'I can't talk to you now,
you've been using.'

'Of course I've fuck'n been using!
I'm a drug addict.'

'It's good to see you're acknowledging it.'

Sanctimonious prick!
'That's why I'm here,
I've come to talk about
my drug addiction.'

'But you know Mal,'
he's speaking slowly now
like I'm some sort of retard.
'You know our policy –
we can't have a counselling session
while you are under the influence.'

'Well, we'll never get to talk then!'
I'm out of there,
slamming doors,
punching the wall.
'Bastards!' I yell.
Pricks!'

Rah rah,
I'm pretty wild and pumped,
but in some part of my brain
I know I might be
a bit difficult to talk to.

Beaten

George got beaten by skinheads.
The rule of the streets is
skinheads beat tramps.
Leave them for dead.
George stopped being a street kid
years ago.

If he was a street kid
they would have raped him.

A sane thought

We don't live well together
without Jess.
Even with her sick in the corner,
we behaved better.

Frank has gone,
so it's just the three of us now,
not enough to survive
in this game.

I call a family meeting
Joe, May and me
sitting around the coffee table.
May, ever the mother, clears a space
pushes the needles and rubbish aside
has found a pen and paper,
like it's a new beginning.

'We can't stay here,' I start off,
'we need to ask others to come
or we'll be pushed out.'
May is making notes
'Who will we ask?' she sucks the end of the pencil,
legs crossed like a secretary.
Joe knows some blokes.
'But if they come we'll never sleep,' he says.

'Why don't we just leave?' I say,
dropping it in like that.

'What?' May stops writing.
They both think I've lost it
which is funny really
because I have.
Here, where we live lost all the time,
we are mad if we have a sane thought.

Answers

May wants to clear out,
says she wants to find her boy.
She thinks he's one now.
It makes her sad,
she's stoned most of the time.

We walk the streets
She holds my hand.
'Mal,' she says,
'You're a good friend,
you never even came on to me.'
I blush like I'm some sort of young kid.

'I'm going to leave,' she says,
stopping in the street, looking at me.
For once she is clear,
her dark face serious,
the street lights making shadows in her frown.

Her gaze follows the street,
up past Parliament House.
'Do you think we'll make it?'
she asks the heavy air.
I don't answer.

Weight of tears

I
The path
is wet paper
and needles
I almost don't notice.
I walk between the gravestones
looking for Jess.
She is here somewhere
lost to me.

II
A memory of love
pulls at me like pain.
I don't cry
but sometimes
my eyes ache
from the weight
of tears.

Chapter 6

The black staircase | August

Payback

It's raining when they appear,
like ghosts walking out of the dark.

One hits me hard.
He's concrete,
I'm folding fresh,
weak and soft.
I fall.
I curl my body tight
but nothing will help.

A piece of wood smashes my balls,
another at my face.
I say I'm sorry!
I lie, I confess.
I almost don't feel the knife.
And when I am quiet,
they stop.

Staircase

I'm following
the black staircase
into the dark,
it looks so real.

Not again

'Josh is that you?
'Josh?
Where are you?'

The yellow light shakes
like it's timid.
Like it's afraid of the dark too.
The voices in my head are a comfort.
Mum is here tonight,
her voice is yellow.
'Josh?'
This time I try to look around,
the voice is so clear,
I think she must be
at the back of the house,
the kitchen most probably.

'Mum?' I start to get up,
and fall.
The ground is a hard bed
wet, black with my blood.

Shit, not again.

Through the dark

Then Bobby's there.
He nudges me with his foot.
I try and talk
but it bubbles out my mouth
and there's only blood.

'Get up Mal,
you fuckwit! Quick!'
And I am up
trying to walk,
his face falling into blackness,
just the white spots of his eyes and teeth
pull me
through the dark.

Blood

I follow him through the park
in a numb stagger.
My smashed face
runs blood,
in thick
rivers down my cheeks
and off my chin.
It stinks.

'Com'on!' he calls,
well ahead of me now
and fast disappearing into the gloom.

I can hear my breath
loud in the quiet.
I keep my eyes on his shadow,
he is like the dead walking.

'Hey! Bobby come back!'
My body hurts,
and the blood spreads down my front
like a pool of black oil in the dark.

Aunty

'Hey! Aunty, this is 'im.'
I see him pointing me out,
not far to go now.

Bastard, he knows I'm hurt
So much for the caring blackfella ways
he's always going on about.

'My mob will help,' he'd said
then he's off
walking – running.

'Hey Mal! here's my mob.'
but then I fall,
fall on someone,
'Hey what you doing man!'
They push me off,
but it's alright now
the pain goes as I black out.

His mob are drinking,
I wake to noise
– a fight?
'Fuck! Bobby I need to go, my nose is smashed,
I can't breathe.'
'Nah, you right, my mob
they got you, hey Aunty!
this bastard's sick.'
'No Bobby,'

I'm waking up now
heading away from the rabble,
then his aunty has my arm,
pushing me to the ground.
She wipes my face,
talks like a mother.
'You poor bastard,'
she says, all caring.
'We fix you up,
stay with us mob, you safe now.'

Great, I think, safe with a smashed face
a fucked body.
My breath pulls in rasps.
I fall again
into blackness,
the roots of the fig
like giant snakes, winding safety
and rough kindness around me.

Vivisection

This dream is about
dismantling things.

I pull back
the skin of my hand
layer upon layer
to find sinew –
pearly white
before blood
rushes from the muscle.

Strangely, this
doesn't hurt.

I watch my inside colours –
purple, blue.
Red ropes of tubes
that should sustain me.

My mind silences my voice,
engulfing me
in a hollow scream.

The gardens

I stay in the gardens for a week.
Aunty washes my face
my cuts
mostly she talks.
'Where's you mother?'
'Gone,' I say
'Passed away?'
Her mouth turns down at the edges like creased paper,
her eyes sad.
Her soft flesh brown and scarred,
but her face is an act of kindness.

Nowhere boy

'You gotta go back to your family.'
Aunty's looking hard at me,
so close I smell grog
and something else.
Her breath sweet and bitter
all at once.
'Go now, it's gotta be now.'

Bobby looks at me hard too,
'That mob comin' back
they know you here now,
make it bad for us.'
'I know Bobby,
that's fine
I'll go.'

Late at night

In the day it's peaceful.
Just the council workers
who care for the garden,
the way people should be cared for.

But it's all action
after dark.
Word is they're coming,
and we prepare for war,
by taking what drugs we have.

The skinheads push through the young blokes
who don't have a hope against the tide of hate,
fighting until they fell
splintered and pulped.
– slowly the cops come
thank god, it was going to be me next.
And by the morning
Bobby's gone
and Aunty is crying.
And there's screaming
all around
the snaking tree roots.

Chapter 7

Taking in the light |
September

My name

The cops find me
the next day
and I'm wasted.
It's lucky they came really –
the rainbows in my eyes
had turned to creatures.

'Hey you, what's your name?'
The cop's head morphs into a dragon
I only remember screaming
as he got me.

'Sick of picking up these pricks!'
They're talking in the front seat
then at me –
'Don't you dare throw up!'

Dark trees rush past the car.
I tried to make them stop
but they don't.

Cops drop me off at juvie.
'State your name and address,'
a grey uniform barks at me.
I obey, anything for peace.

'My name is Josh Mallard,
I'm known as Malcolm.
I'm from nowhere'

Taking in the light

'Bloody kids!'
As he yells his lip curls up on the left,
his breath stinks,
and spit flies out
of his mouth.
'Where are your parents?'
I worry I might catch something from him,
but any move I make
is an act of aggression.

I watch his red face
think about the light again
how strange the light is,
how grey it is.

I want to tell him this,
ask where Bobby and Aunty are,
but it is too hard to talk.

I try and tell them about the guy in the lane,
it was dark, there was no light,
he was too close,
I didn't mean to hurt him.
The memory is of dark corners,
fear, blood,
thick black blood
taking all the light.

Juvie

It's like a motel
only someone else signs me in
and the door is locked from the outside.
Room service is limited
and you shit where you eat.

Strange though –
I sleep better than I have for months.

I'm working my way through
Government institutions.

Did you know
they all smell the same,
and disinfectant doesn't mask
the smell of shit?

Pain dream

The dream forces me to wake.
Streetlights like yellow moons glare at me,
smudged through high windows.
The city is silent and grey.

The pain crushes at me
and I feel for blood, broken bones,
but when I recall a fragment of dream.

It was the pain
that helped me make things,
fix things.
I used the pain to save Jess,
to wake Mum.
To find May.

I used the pain to build a car,
it was a Lego car.
Like I'm little again.
Joining each piece
hurt so much,
I writhed on the floor.
Until I had it,
something to escape in.

Awake

I
I'm awake.
It's three days now.
No sleep
makes the world shine.

II
In the hospital they take my clothes,
all my things.
I sit day and night in a gown
and flash my arse to the world.
Grandad said this place would help.

'How is this meant to help?' I yell,
'I'm fuck'n freezing.'

The counsellor says,
'Malcolm, you're here
because you're not well.
We need to protect you.'
These conversations always end up
with me being be silent.

I wonder what God thinks.
Then I wonder why God is silent?

The counsellor is working up to a question,
so I say,
'I have to go to the toilet now.'

His questions would keep.

Taking me home

I'm getting used to
rooms that smell of puke.
And scratches in the wall,
Road to Hell
Ring Sharon 0404144328
Jesus is the answer
AN was here only one!
I don't need to add more.

The worker comes in.
'Hey Mal, your grandfather is here,
he's come to take you home.'

Grandad

When I wake the sun is shining
the light fills
the room
and I wonder
where I've been.

Grandad looked sad
like someone has hurt him
or someone has died.
I thought it could be me
because the light looks wrong.

'Hey Grandad?'
He jumps.
'Malcolm?'
His hand is in mine
and he smiles,
and that old face
folded into lines
as the smile travels up
to his eyes.

I'm related to this old man,
how is good is that?

Spring

The wind is light
laden with air from somewhere else.
I go out,
walk the streets down
by Grandad's
past green gardens.

I stick to the road
away from the trees
where drifting homeless lives collide
and crash.

Jasmine rests on the air
above the grey
and I let
my numbed
sense of smell
come back.

Court

'You're in a bit of trouble son.'
The judge looks down on me
like he's god.

I don't say anything.

'I can see you've had family problems.'

I don't say anything.

'What are we going to do with you?'

I feel like saying fuck off
but I don't.

'You have been before the juvenile court before.'

He frowns at me
and his eyes disappear under thick eyebrows
like I have let him down.

Good behaviour

Don't know how it happened
but I got a good behaviour bond.

Must be some advantages
in having a fucked-up family.

Jennifer

'I'm Jennifer, the Court Liaison Officer.'
she holds out her hand to me,
I take it numbly.

'I'm here to help you
get a place to live, to sort out rehab.'

The world tips slightly,
and my hands fly up as I steady myself.

'We can discuss work too.
If you like, or study.
I hear you did well at school.'

I stop hearing her voice,
stop listening.
I just see her looking at me.
She's here to help me
and I think –
this is a good moment.

Records

I know she's got my records,
been through them,
knows more about my family than I do.

I hate that she knows stuff I don't.

She doesn't talk about it though.

'How's your day?' she asks.
'Are you staying safe?' she asks.

And I wonder
if she was
once homeless too.

Trying too hard

'What music do you like Josh?'
'Mal,' I say.
'Ok Mal, what music do you like?'

She's different, this woman
not your usual support worker type.

'Dunno,' I say.
'Come on Mal, I know you've got an iPod.'

'Well what do you listen to?' I say.
'Oh, very good, Mal, clever, ok let me think.
I like The Waifs, The Audreys...'
'I've heard of The Waifs, my mum...' I let slip.

'You listen to The Waifs?' she jumps in.
'No I've *heard* of them.'
'They've got a Josh in their band,' she says.

Don't try too hard, I think, shutting down.

The other side

Dear Malcolm,
I'm writing this
so you get it after I'm gone.
In the end I was glad I left.
The cops said you'd gone to prison
for that stabbing,
but the ice freak told me about the hospital.

I'm pretty much had it now,
like Jess, can't eat or sleep.
I feel like I see dead people
walking around.
I figure if I can see them
I'm nearly there.

Mostly I'm sad –
was sort of hoping for more.
I'm sorry
we didn't get
to the hills
like we talked about.
Always know
that I love you.
May.

Going straight

This is why
I've been stoned for years,
it hurts knowing.

Hills

The air is like ice
on my skin.
Here I can see the distance
until the air fades.
The colours are pale,
thinning at the edges.

I'm alone again
but it's good this time.
My choice you could say,
but I'm here for May and Jess,
for the mob.

The city floats
miles from here
trapped in its own noise and filth
like a growling animal.

I can see it all now
and I wonder why it took me
so long to leave.

Port Philip Prison

I made Grandad come.
He told me he didn't care
if he never saw the bastard again,
then he shrugged,
'But he's your father.'

Heavy metal doors open
like the ones in my dream,
and we sit in a room
painted yellow and blue,
to make us feel better.

We wait for an age.
Grandad starts to pace.
It's so long I forget to be afraid.
But when a door
in the distance bangs,
the fear is there again
frothing out of me.

The man they bring in is shorter
than I remember,
he is frowning though.
I remember that.

The officer stays.
Stands against the wall
hands behind his straight back.

'Hi,' I say.
'Hi,' he says as he sits.
Grandad says nothing.

'Why'd you come?'
my father says to me.

What I wanted to happen

'I've had a hard time, I tell him,
but I'm getting better now
with Grandad's help.'
I imagine a scowl.

'Just thought I'd come and see you.
You know, the counsellor
thought I should,
but I don't have to come again,
once is enough.

I see not much has changed for you
and that's crap really,
because I've been fucked up for years.
You never knew how to care for me.
But that's ok I'm over it now.'

We sit in silence
because what's the point?

I imagine hear him muttering something.
"What?' I say,
What's that?'

His head is down.
'You look like her,' he says,
and when I look again
I imagine he's crying.

Chapter 8

Darwin | December

The park

It must be a good week.
I meet a bloke who plays footy
with his little brother
in the park.

I'm trying to practice talking
'regular' as George would put it.
He told me normal people have 'interests.'

'These would be things you do
that are acceptable.'

George also told me
 I have to appear interested
in what people are saying.

I told George he's a fine one to be coaching me.
'I said 'appear interested' didn't I?' he answers,
right when I think he's not listening.

I try out George's idea on this bloke.
Find out he's into fitness,
rides his bike every weekend.
'Right' I say.

They ask me to play with them
and I run around like a mad thing,
remembering what it was like.

I'm tired at the end
and they say they'll be here
again tomorrow if I want have a kick.

I'd like to tell George I've found
an acceptable interest.

Hanging out

My room overlooks a park.
From my front window
I see people walking by,
hanging out.

A girl lies in the same spot
each day reading a book.

Because I've got nothing to do
I go to the park,
wait for my new football friends.

She see me looking at her
at what she's reading,
and I'm embarrassed to be sprung.
I smile so she's not frightened
then I remember my smile
looks like a grimace.

'You live around here don't you?'
She's talking like I'm a rabbit
that's easily startled.

'Yeah,' and before I can stop myself,
I point at the share house.

'I live in that box over there.'
She points to the other side of the park.
'It's freezing, so I come here to warm up.
I'm studying English Lit at Melbourne Uni.
I'm Rachel.'

'I'm Malcolm,' I say, extending my hand.
I'm pleased I can have a conversation.
She's lovely too, this girl,
open and friendly.

'I've seen your friends
come and go, looks like
a busy place.'

'It can be,
and they're probably not friends
just housemates,'
trying to make light of it.
I don't tell her we are all fresh from rehab.

'Is that why you're in the park?'

'Yeah and I'm bored,
I don't have a job.'

'That must be hard.'

'Do you have many people in your house?'
I ask to change the subject.

'Four of us, all at uni,
studying for exams.
So it's boring,
and cold.'

Rachel starts packing up,
'Well, good to meet you,
hope you find a job.'

'Thanks Rachel,
see you round.'

Then she's gone.

Shadows

Afterwards,
I wondered if it was a dream.

Like I'd floated
on a black lake,
a speck of dust
on its surface.

My life some sort of bad joke
threatening to end,
over and over,

and all those
floating alongside me
were only ever shadows.

Darwin

Later, when I'm well again,
I go up north.
Like I always wanted to do
with Mum.

Grandad comes with me. He's old
but I've started to think he'd live forever.

We travel by train,
taking in days of endless red sand
until the country drops away
into a flat green sea
that becomes the horizon.

The train took us through each valley and sand dune,
to a place where no one from my family had ever lived.

The folklore of my childhood tells me otherwise
and stories that didn't happen fill photo albums,
bright pictures of me with Dad, fishing.
Two of us happily holding up our prize catch for Mum,
dopey grins, sunny under floppy hats.
It's all there – and not, in a heartbeat.

It's the wet season in Darwin
and the mouldy air's thick
sucking at my lungs.
The harbour lies like wet concrete,
still and silent inside the curve of the bay.

On a grey dawn
I pour Mum's ashes
on the still water and say goodbye.
Grandad sings a song for her
in an old language,
and drops white frangipanis in the water.
We watch them drift
in the smudge of ash
The sun comes up
yellow and blinding from behind heavy cloud.

I have her journal with me
and read one of her poems to the air,
I hope she can hear me.

Postscript for May

Heavy mist falls close
and the day darkens.
The place is huge, old,
a convent, it says on the gate
which makes me smile.
And in the still quiet,
the gravel crunches
under my feet.

I've come for May,
to see her at least,
and when she's in my arms
I wonder why I waited so long,
what I was afraid of?

We're older, more serious,
her frown is deeper, dark rings under her eyes,
but when she laughs
her young face comes back.

'So?' she smiles.
'So what?' I say, my eyes locked on hers.
'Well, what now – now you know
I'm a loony?'

'You're not mad, you're in rehab,
and they reckon you're almost better.
And, if you want to,
when you get out,

you can come and stay
with Grandad and me –
only if you want to.'

She's crying but I'm ready for it this time.

'And May...'
She's drying her eyes, sniffing,
'What Mal, why are you looking at me like that?'
I hold her small hands in mine,
my fingers brush her scarred dark arms.

'May, I've found your little boy.'

Author's note

The first poem written for the verse novel *Malcolm* was scribbled on the last day of a writing workshop with playwright Jenny Kemp, in the bright airy studios of the School of Drama at the Victorian College of the Arts on St Kilda Road in Melbourne.

'Jess's dream' arrived from the pen almost as it appears now. It was the last day of the workshop and I'd made a pact with myself to read something out to the group. All week I had listened to the work of an inspiring group of playwrights, actors and drama teachers. I was in awe of their openness and their ability to put their work out there. As a poet, more used to quiet writing spaces and stolen moments of thought that grow into a poem, it was liberating to read 'Jess's dream' aloud and I knew from their response I was onto something.

Riding the train out of the city at the end of the day, I composed another ten poems. I couldn't write fast enough, they poured from me, my pen in rhythm with the train, the hour-long trip over too quickly. I'd just begun, but already I had to change pace. Just when the story had started to unfurl, I had to go back to my life in Alice Springs.

'Jess's dream' gave me the opening into Malcolm's story. It introduced the voice of Malcolm and the directness of his speech. It also introduced me to the character of Jess, who is pivotal to the story. She is the friend who comes with Malcolm from his early teens at school into the uncharted territory of this story. As much as this story is about Malcolm, it is also about Jess. Her demise is his, too, and the loss of Jess is the catalyst that forces a change in Malcolm.

Stories arise from deep places, from personal experience and from memory. This one has also come from years working as a nurse in city hospitals and in remote settings in central Australia, and after five years of teaching at the Alice Springs prison.

My time working in the prison system is the background but not the source of the story. None of the characters in Malcolm are drawn from any one person, but rather from years of listening. In the prison I worked with men who lived with dysfunction. Lives fractured by drugs, alcohol, an inadequate education system, and the trauma of disruption to traditional culture and language. I taught English literacy and creative writing to students with a limited ability to express themselves in the written form. The majority of my students were Aboriginal men, drawn from all over the Northern Territory and northern Australia, many of whom spoke English as their fourth or fifth language. Just a handful of these men could read and write in their first language.

By studying creative writing and literacy, my students started writing down their stories, and they had great stories to tell. They told me how driving fast through the night, drunk and stoned, especially if being chased by the cops, made them feel like they were flying. They told me the order they'd take drugs in, so that when they went out on the town, they'd make the most of speed and alcohol, making the effects last as long as possible. They told me that their anger led them to do so many things they regretted. They told me how the cops treated them like shit, and I watched as prison officers made grown men feel like dirt.

I listened to stories of drug deals and beatings gone wrong. Of robberies and car-jackings, of hiding out in the bush, from police, from payback. And I listened as men told me over and over that it wasn't their fault, that the judge and jury got it wrong, that the lawyer was a bastard and didn't do his job properly, that they were doing it harder than anyone else, that other blokes got it easy.

Many of the men told me how much they loved their children. Photographs of their children were used as bookmarks and produced regularly to show anyone who would listen how much they missed them. I felt deep sadness for their loss. And sadness for the irony of the situation; that they loved their children but by being in prison they didn't have to do anything about it. Often life was easier for their children not having them around because their violence and alcohol or drug use was problematic when they were home, causing disruption and trauma in the children's lives.

By studying writing, though, they started to read, discuss books and write poetry and stories. Some went on to be published and to perform their work outside the prison. Some finished their sentences and left the prison.

It was against this background that the character of Malcolm emerged. In the end, the story of Malcolm is about the families of prisoners – the partners and the children of prisoners, who are the real victims. Families of convicted prisoners need help, the children whose lives are thrown into turmoil by the actions of unthinking or damaged parents need attention. These stories need to come into the light. If those of us who have witnessed this damage unfolding do not speak out, who will?

Malcolm could have been prose, a play, a film or a documentary. But really it was always going to be poetry and through narrative verse I could write about Malcolm, a young man I have never met but who I know intimately.

Acknowledgements

This story first came to light under the expert teaching and care of playwright Jenny Kemp. The Generative Skills workshops that she runs have provided extraordinary creative support for my writing which I am constantly grateful for.

Over the years of its development, *Malcolm* has benefited from the feedback of writers and poets who generously read the work and offered suggestions. I acknowledge with deep gratitude the late Deb Westbury, whose wisdom and generosity guided the writing during a four-week residency in the Blue Mountains. This story is dedicated to her memory. Janet Hutchinson provided invaluable editing at a number of stages as the story grew. My thanks to Varuna – The National Writers House for a Dorothy Hewett Poetry Fellowship in 2009, for nurturing this story and my writing over many years and, most recently, a Residential Fellowship in 2019.

The work has been developed as a theatre script with generous support and direction from playwright Mary Anne Butler and dramaturge Peter Matheson, and performed at Araluen Arts Centre in Alice Springs as part of the Red Hot Arts Bite Size Theatre program. An excerpt was performed at Wordstorm Writers' Festival in Darwin, May 2010, and at La Trobe University, Melbourne, in September 2010. An early version of this work was written as part of the Master's program at Central Queensland University.

The support of the writing community in Alice Springs sustains my writing. My thanks go to Jo Dutton who has believed in this story from the moment she first read an excerpt. My thanks, too, to Sue Fielding and Meg Mooney for their support and for being close readers of my poetry, and to Shari Kocher for her thoughtful feedback. To Jenny Pechey, whose friendship has sustained me throughout the many years of living in central Australia.

I am grateful to my extended family for reading early drafts of the work. To my parents, David and Merle U'Ren, for their love and acceptance; to my darling siblings, your inspirational impact on the world has influenced this story. And to Joan Shilton, who is a constant supporter of my poetry.

To my children, who are such stunning adults, you have taught me how to notice the world. Thank you for your belief in *Malcolm* and for your insightful feedback. My deep love and thanks to Chris, who has watched this story grow out of me; your patience and love have helped to give *Malcolm* a voice.

Finally, my gratitude to my publisher, Terri-ann White, and the incredible team at UWA Publishing, for their belief and support in getting *Malcolm* onto the page and into the world.